Alex Alligator ate apples and apricots in the afternoon.

Ben, the Baboon, bought a big bicycle on his brother's birthday.

Carol Caterpillar cut a cake and crawled on the carpet to watch a cartoon clip.

D

Dainty Diana, Daddy's darling daughter loves delicious doughnuts.

Elma Egret got into the elevator to see an eagle sitting on an elephant, eating an egg.

F

Fat Freddie Frog fell on the floor.

Gracie Goat got a
great gift from her granny.

H

Harry Horse has a
huge hare on his hat.

Ila's pet Incy Iguana loves ice cream
who loves ice cream.

J

Jack, the Jaguar and Jill,
the Jackal live in the jungle.

K

Katy
Kangaroo
loves to fly
kites.

L

Linda Lioness
loves lettuce,
lamb chops
and lollipops.

M

Maria Monkey's mommy made
a magic mat for her moppet.

Nelly Nightingale never returns
to her nest before noon.

Olof Ocelot ate an orange and an omelette and was off to meet Olive Octopus.

Pamela Pigeon put her pen and pencil
in the pink pouch and left for the party.

Q

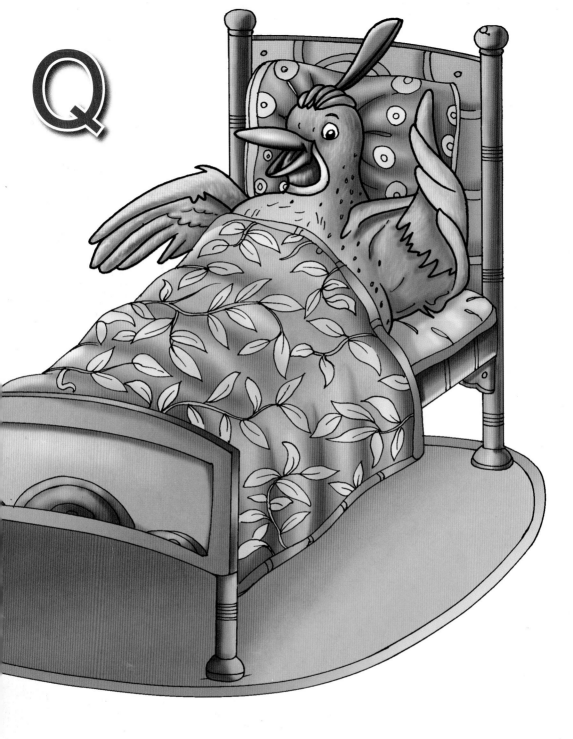

Queeny Quail has a
quilt which keeps her
quite warm.

R

Ronnie Rabbit
ran a race with
Rocky the Ram.

S

Spider Sam sat
sipping strawberry
juice on a sunny,
Sunday morning.

T

Tiger Tim took
Tambie the
Tortoise and
Taira the teal
for a trek.

U

Umer's Uncle has an ugly Unicorn
under his umbrella.

V

Victor Vulture loves to eat
vegetables and play the violin.

Walter Walrus wore a white
waistcoat and went to work.

Alex fixed a xylophone, put it in a box and gave it as a gift to Max on Xmas.

Yasmine has a yak which eats yam.
It sits near Yasmine's yellow yacht and
yawns all the year round.

Y

Zara Zebra zipped to Zaire to see a chimpanzee and a lizard. Wasn't that crazy?